INTERPRET THIS!
COMMONLY USED
IDIOMS

Vocabulary Skills | Language Arts 5th Grade

Children's ESL Books

BABY PROFESSOR
EDUCATION KIDS

First Edition, 2020

Published in the United States by Speedy Publishing LLC, 40 E Main Street, Newark, Delaware 19711 USA.

© 2020 Baby Professor Books, an imprint of Speedy Publishing LLC

Baby Professor Books are available at special discounts when purchased in bulk for industrial and sales-promotional use. For details contact our Special Sales Team at Speedy Publishing LLC, 40 E Main Street, Newark, Delaware 19711 USA. Telephone (888) 248-4521 Fax: (210) 519-4043. www.speedybookstore.com

10 9 8 7 6 * 5 4 3 2 1

Print Edition: 9781541950719
Digital Edition: 9781541952515

See the world in pictures. Build your knowledge in style.
www.speedypublishing.com

TABLE OF CONTENTS

What is an Idiom?...5
Common Idiom 1 *Spins a yarn*.........................8
Common Idiom 2 *A hot potato*.......................14
Common Idiom 3 *To bite the hand that feeds you*.....18
Common Idiom 4 *Green with envy*....................24
Common Idiom 5 *A piece of cake*....................29
Common Idiom 6 *When pigs fly*.......................35
Common Idiom 7 *Hive of activity*....................40
Common Idiom 8 *Square peg in a round hole or round peg in a square hole*.................44
Common Idiom 9 *Silver lining*........................49
Common Idiom 10 *Born with a silver spoon in his mouth*.................................53
Common Idiom 11 *A slap on the wrist*...............58
Common Idiom 12 *At my wit's end*...................62
Common Idiom 13 *The devil is in the details*...........66
SUMMARY..71

"In this book, we're going to talk about common idioms, so let's get right to it!"

What is an Idiom?

An idiom is a phrase that doesn't mean exactly what it says, but instead stands for something else. Most people know what commonly used idioms mean. They are examples of figurative language, which is language that's used to paint a picture of something with imaginative words. The history of some idioms can be traced back to the first time they were used, but in some cases no one knows where they started.

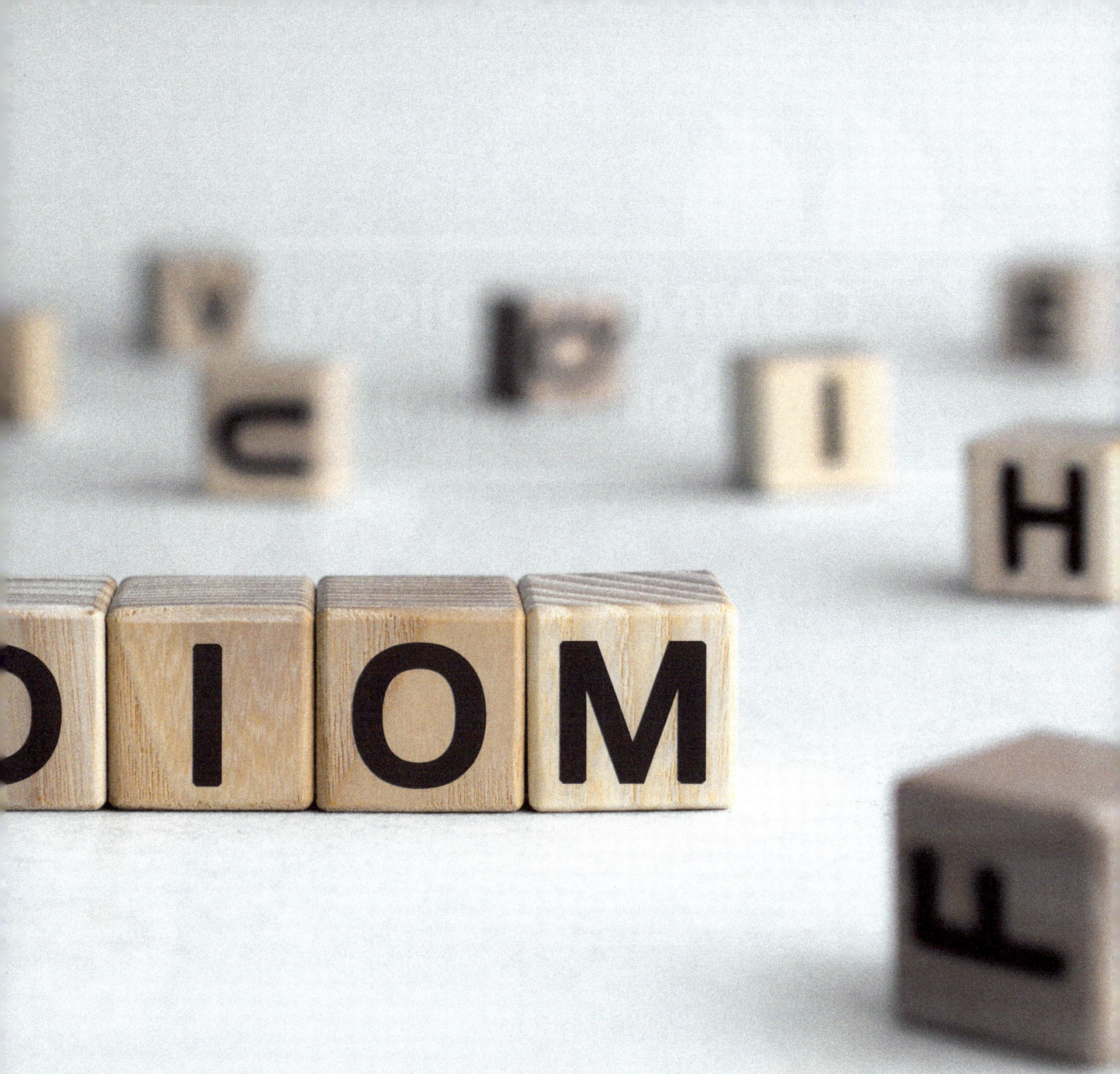
IOM

COMMON IDIOM 1

Spins a yarn

What Does It Mean?

"Spins a yarn" doesn't mean that someone is actually spinning something. It means that the person is telling a story with exaggerated details.

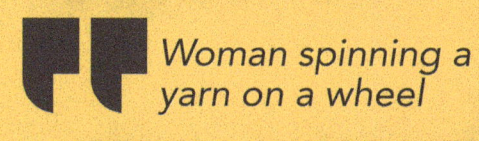
Woman spinning a yarn on a wheel

The story they are telling may be long and somewhat far-fetched. They don't know for sure, but historians believe that the idiom "spinning a yarn" originally came from sailors. The idiom was in print as early as the first part of the nineteenth century, but its exact origin isn't known.

One of the regular tasks on the ship was to repair various ropes. The strands of ropes are called yarns, just like the strands of fibers used in fabric.

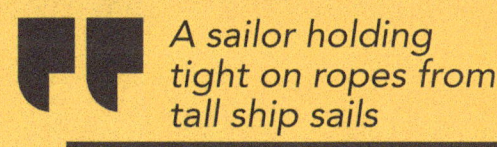
A sailor holding tight on ropes from tall ship sails

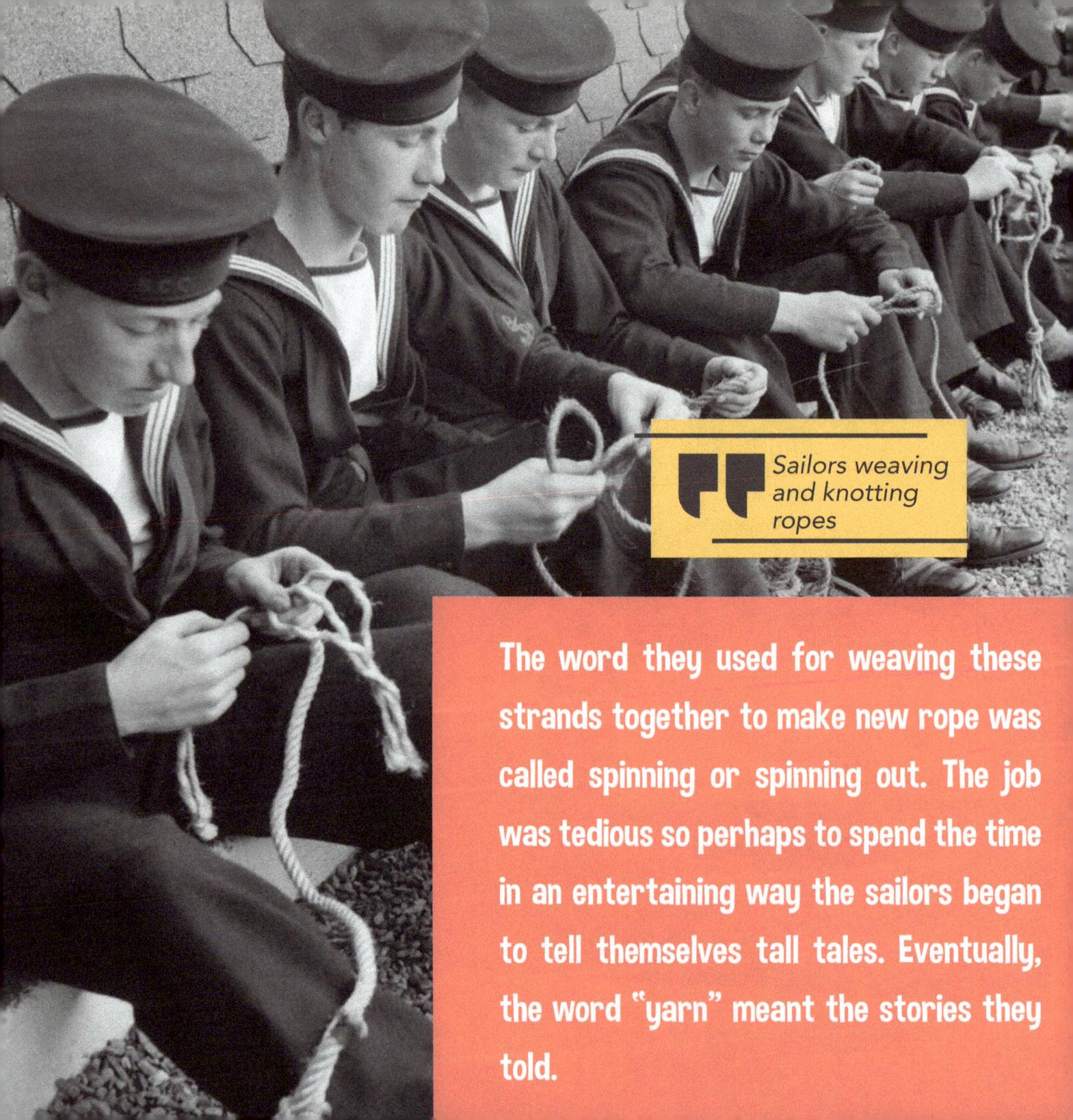

Sailors weaving and knotting ropes

The word they used for weaving these strands together to make new rope was called spinning or spinning out. The job was tedious so perhaps to spend the time in an entertaining way the sailors began to tell themselves tall tales. Eventually, the word "yarn" meant the stories they told.

A Sample Sentence

> " My friend spun a yarn about the size of the whale-like fish he caught. "

COMMON IDIOM 2
A hot potato

What Does It Mean?

The idiom "a hot potato" means something that is risky, sensitive, or difficult to deal with.

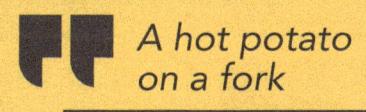
A hot potato on a fork

The phrase started in the middle of the 1800s and came from the expression "drop like a hot potato," which means to drop or abandon something quickly. Potatoes that are cooked in a pot retain their heat so if you pick one up it's hot!

Guy juggling a hot potato in his hands

The subject of whether he should go to college was a hot potato when he visited with his family.

COMMON IDIOM 3
To bite the hand that feeds you

What Does It Mean?

This idiom means to behave badly toward someone who is helping you or providing you with the means to live.

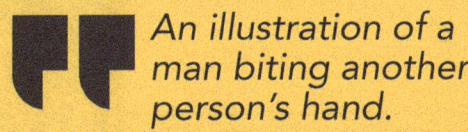

An illustration of a man biting another person's hand.

This phrase may have been around in ancient times, but one of the first references of it in print is from Edmund Burke in a book called Thoughts and Details of Scarcity, which was published in the 18th century.

Edmund Burke

In the book, he's arguing that those people who get a handout from the government are likely to rebel against the government and "bite the hand that feeds them."

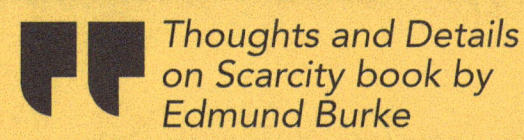
Thoughts and Details on Scarcity book by Edmund Burke

THOUGHTS AND DETAILS ON SCARCITY

EDMUND BURKE

KISSINGER LEGACY REPRINTS

It's easy to see that the phrase more than likely came from the everyday realities of feeding animals on a farm and getting bitten on more than one occasion.

> "He didn't like what his boss was doing, but he didn't protest because he didn't want to bite the hand that fed him."

COMMON IDIOM 4
Green with envy

What Does It Mean?

"Green with envy" means that you are upset that someone else has something valuable that you would like to have.

The lady in the green dress envies the lady in red

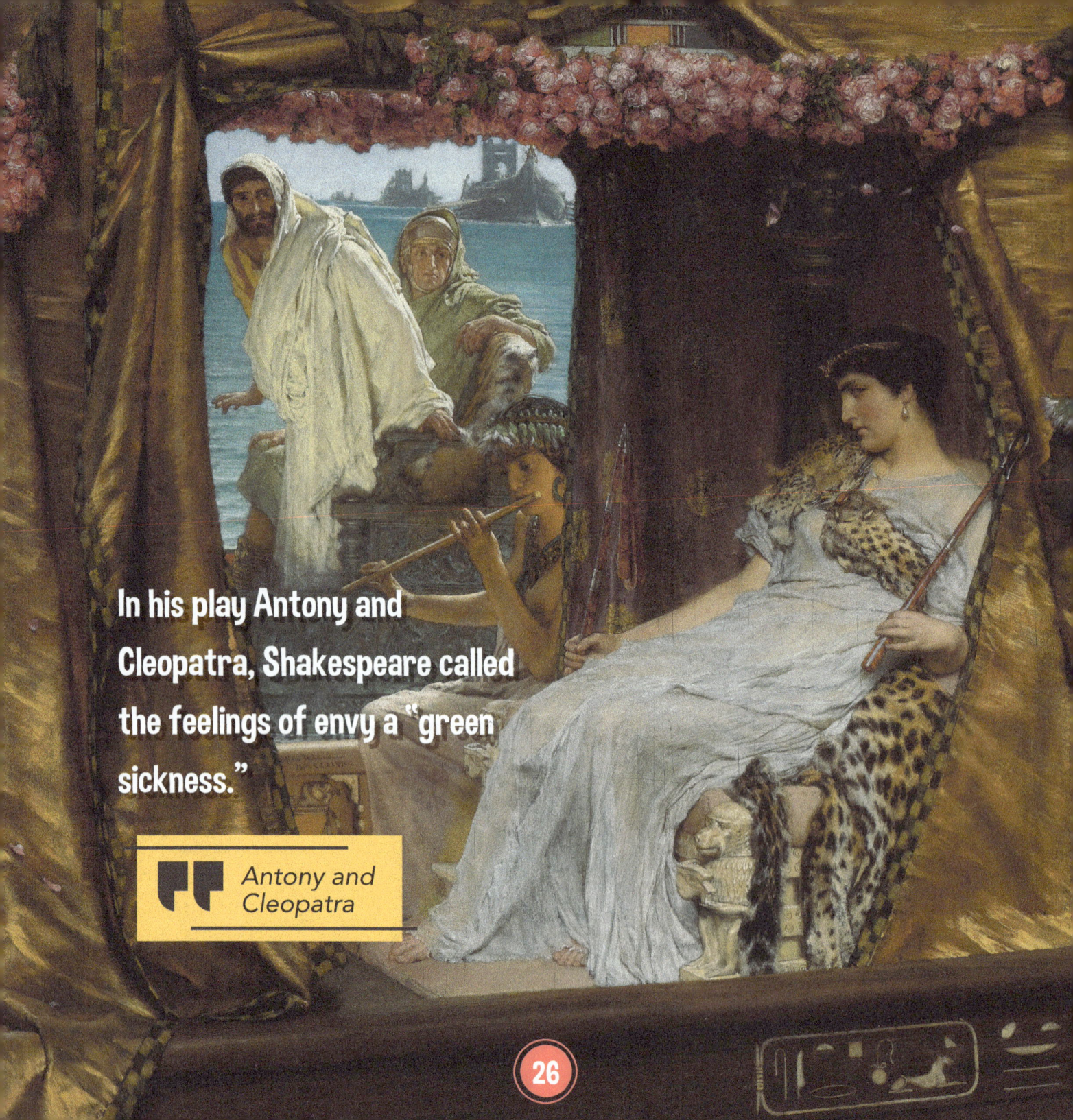

In his play Antony and Cleopatra, Shakespeare called the feelings of envy a "green sickness."

Antony and Cleopatra

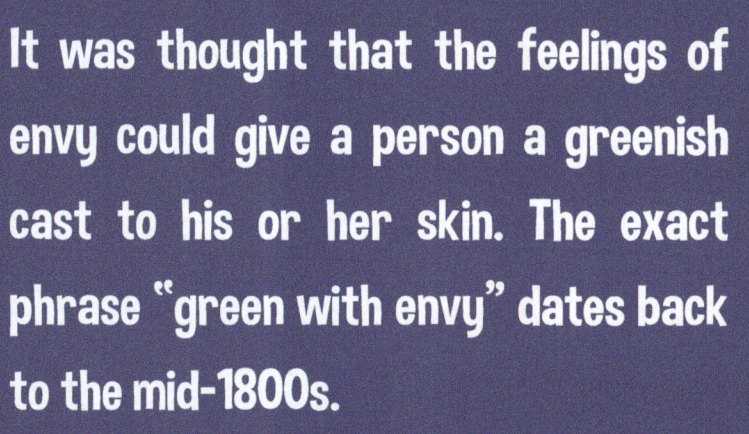

It was thought that the feelings of envy could give a person a greenish cast to his or her skin. The exact phrase "green with envy" dates back to the mid-1800s.

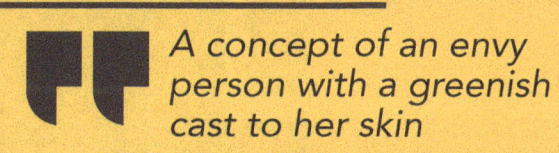
A concept of an envy person with a greenish cast to her skin

A Sample Sentence

"
She was green with envy
when she found out I was
vacationing in Paris.
"

COMMON IDIOM 5
A piece of cake

What Does It Mean?

The idiom "a piece of cake" means that a particular action is easy or fun to do.

A piece of cake

The word "easy" was first associated with cake in the 1870s. At that time, cakes were distributed as prizes when people would win a competition.

You get a cake if you win in a contest in the 1870s

In states that had slavery, there was a cake ceremony during celebrations. Slaves would encircle a cake during the event and the couple that was the most graceful would win the cake.

Cake Walk, 1896

"Cake walk" is another idiom that means the same thing. In 1936, the famous poet Ogden Nash used the idiom "a piece of cake" in one of his printed poems.

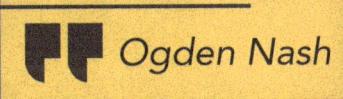 Ogden Nash

A Sample Sentence

> He thought the test would be difficult, but instead he found that making an A was a piece of cake.

COMMON IDIOM 6
When pigs fly

What Does It Mean?

The idiom "when pigs fly" means something that is impossible or will never happen. People usually use a tone of sarcasm or humor when using it.

It comes from a Scottish proverb that is many centuries old, but in American literature there's a famous reference to it in Lewis Carroll's book Alice in Wonderland.

The cover of Alice's Adventures in Wonderland, written by Lewis Carroll

In the story, the Duchess tells Alice that she has as much right to think on her own as a pig has to fly. In other words, Alice doesn't have the right to think on her own at all!

Alice and the Duchess

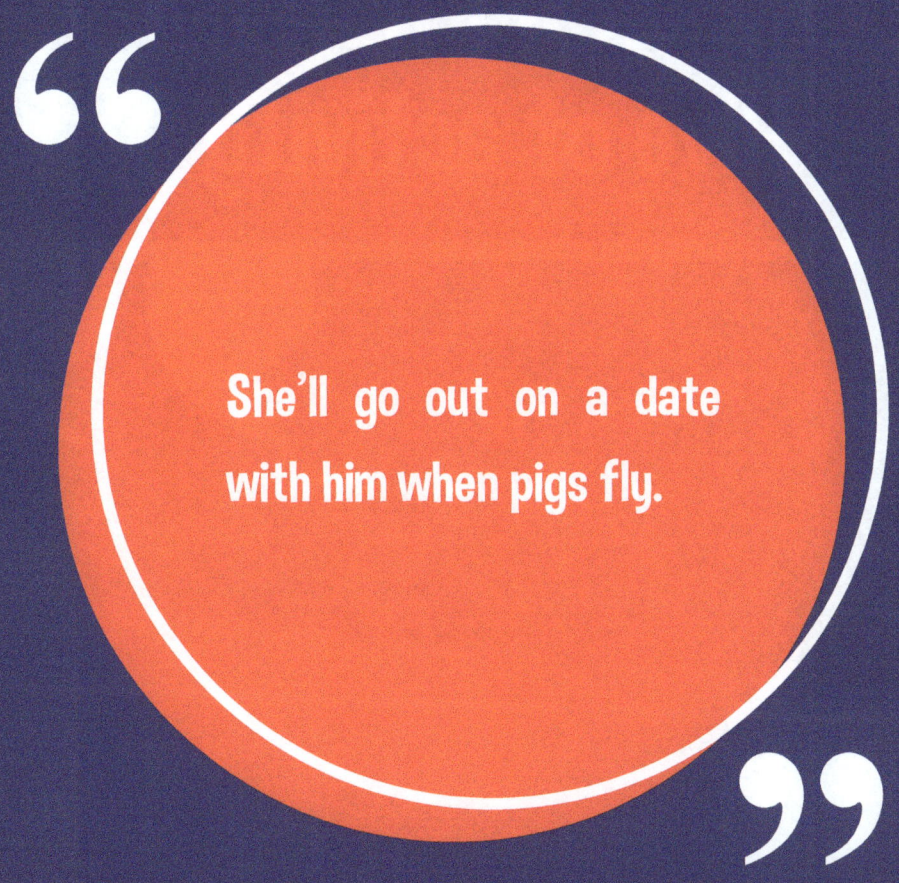

"She'll go out on a date with him when pigs fly."

COMMON IDIOM 7
Hive of activity

What Does It Mean?

If you've ever seen a bee hive, you'll quickly understand what this idiom means. It simply means a location where there's lots of activity going on.

A honey bee box with a hive inside

No one knows exactly when this idiom was started, but its image is unmistakable.

A bunch of bees on a honeycomb in a hive

"

The school was a hive of activity a week before the holiday vacation.

"

COMMON IDIOM 8
Square peg in a round hole or round peg in a square hole

What Does It Mean?

This idiom simply means that a person doesn't fit a specific situation. The person's personality or actions are awkward for the situation in question. He or she might not be comfortable.

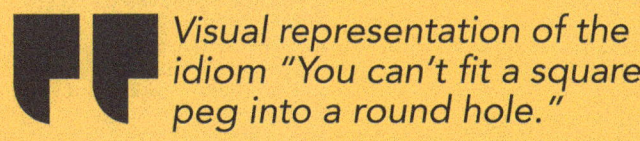

Visual representation of the idiom "You can't fit a square peg into a round hole."

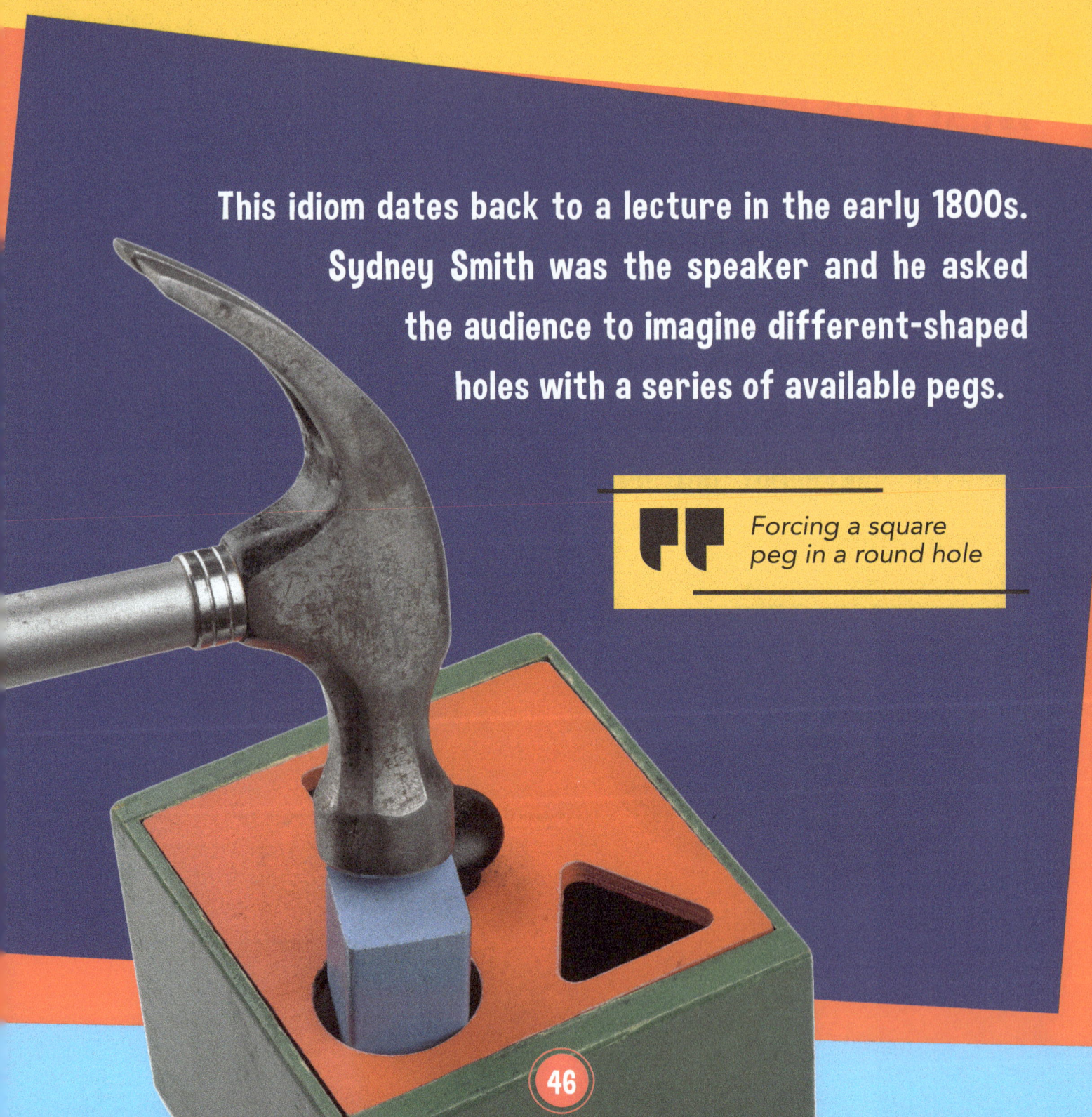

This idiom dates back to a lecture in the early 1800s. Sydney Smith was the speaker and he asked the audience to imagine different-shaped holes with a series of available pegs.

Forcing a square peg in a round hole

He told the audience that it would be rare for the correct peg to be matched with the correct hole.

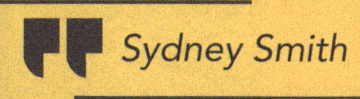 *Sydney Smith*

A Sample Sentence

> "
> He tried to fit in at the party, but he felt like a square peg in a round hole.
> "

COMMON IDIOM 9
Silver lining

What Does It Mean?

This idiom comes from a longer well-known phrase "every cloud has a silver lining."

A Silver lining

It's believed to have originated from the writings of the famous author John Milton in 1634 when he talked about a sable cloud turning forth a silver lining on the night.

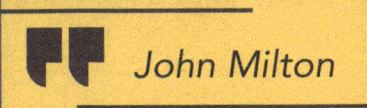

John Milton

A Sample Sentence

He lost his job, but the silver lining was he had time to write his first best-selling book.

Born with a silver spoon in his mouth

What Does It Mean?

The idiom "born with a silver spoon in his mouth" means that the person in question was born wealthy.

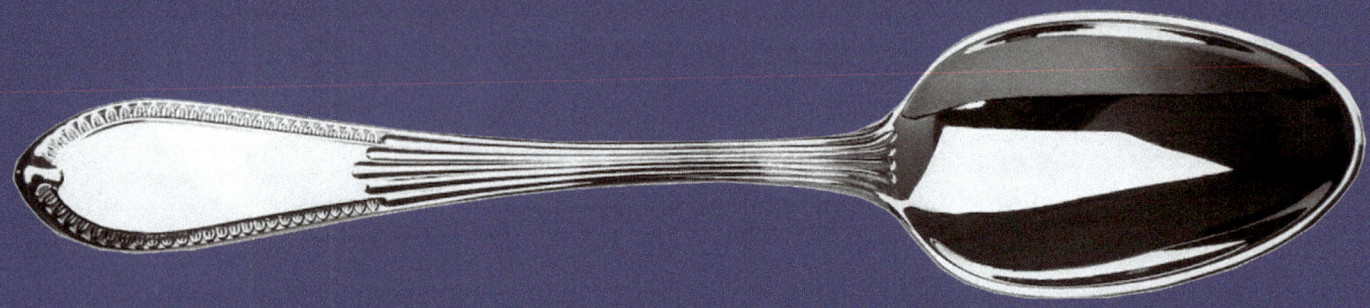

A Silver Spoon

It's believed that this idiom started in England and referred to British aristocrats. It was common for well-to-do godparents to give gifts of silver spoons to their godchildren during christening ceremonies.

British aristocrats

The first time this idiom appeared in print was in the United States in 1801. It appeared in a Congressional publication that mentioned few lawyers were "born with silver spoons in their mouths."

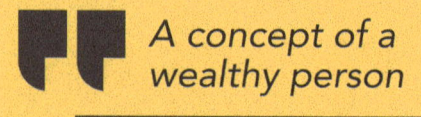

A concept of a wealthy person

"

She wore inexpensive clothes so no one knew she was born with a silver spoon in her mouth.

"

COMMON IDIOM 11
A slap on the wrist

What Does It Mean?

The idiom "a slap on the wrist" means that a penalty wasn't very harsh. It's more than likely that this idiom evolved during 18th century England.

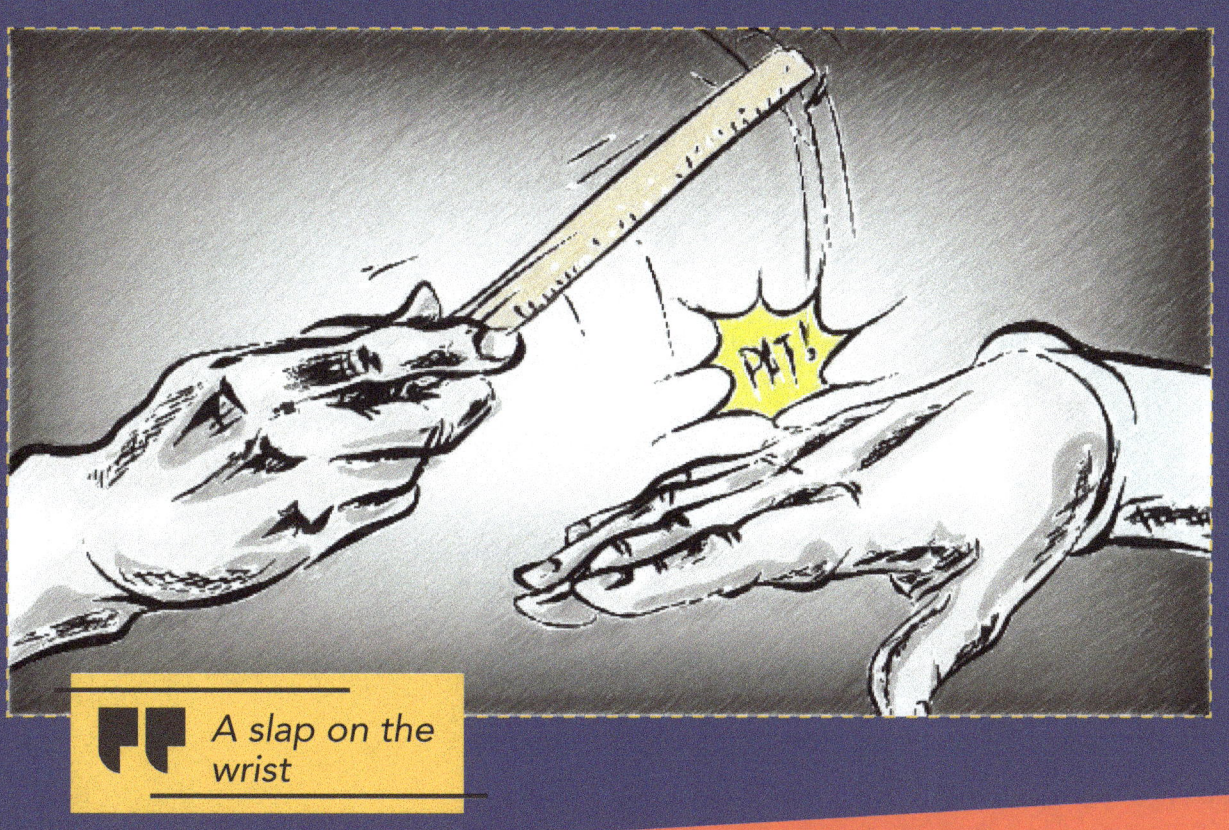

A slap on the wrist

During that time there were harsh punishments for crimes and the word "slap" began to take on a different meaning than its true definition. "A slap on the wrist" would be very minor compared to most punishments.

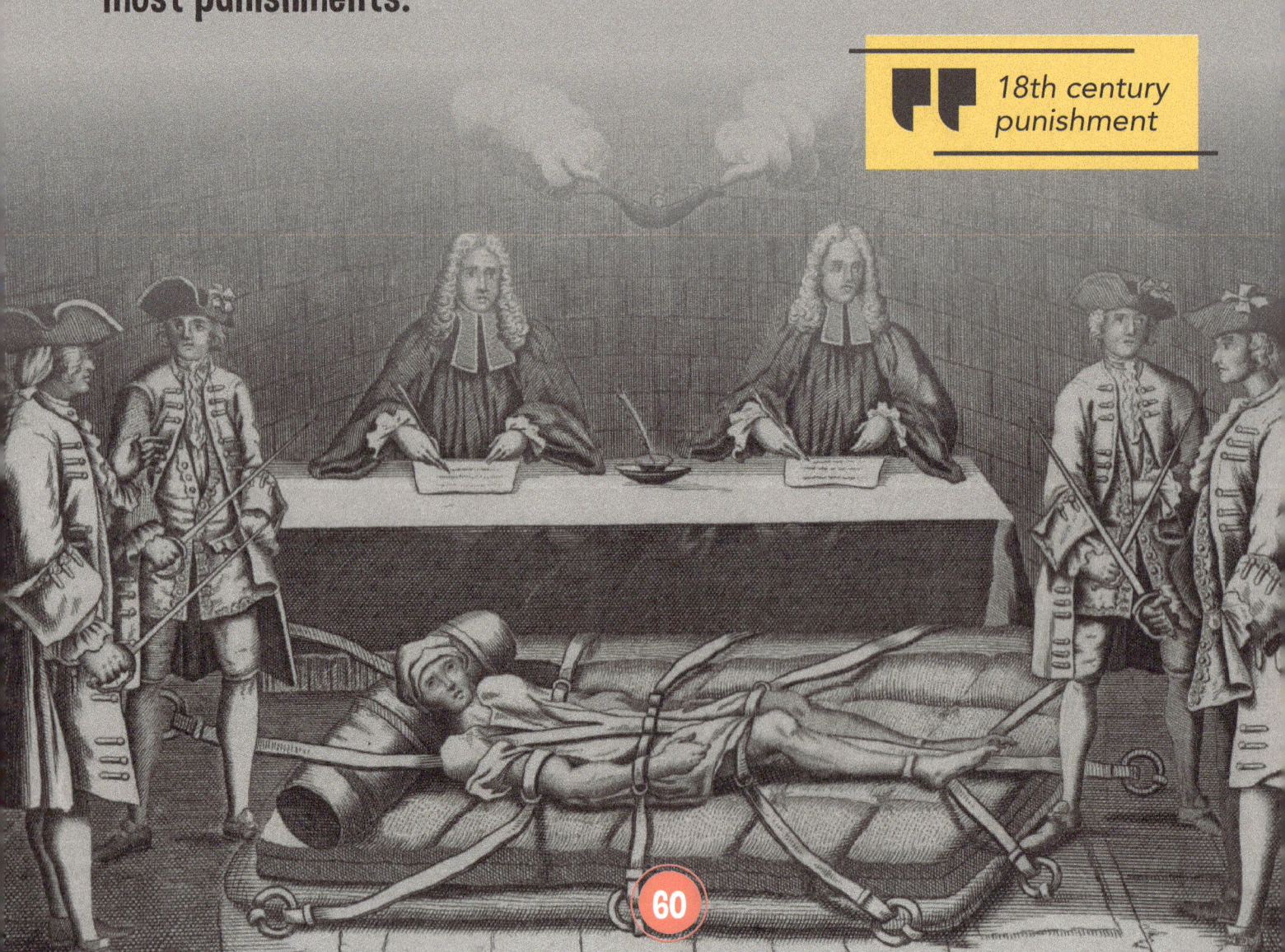

18th century punishment

" She thought James would be thrown in jail, but the judge's decision was just a slap on the wrist. "

COMMON IDIOM 12
At my wit's end

What Does It Mean?

The idiom "at my wit's end" means that you've exhausted your ability to deal with something.

An image of a frustrated man

This idiom first appeared in a poem written in 1377 in Middle English. The poem is called Piers Plowman and it was written by William Langland. By wit, Langland didn't mean sparkling conversation. Instead he was talking about a state of mind- the ability to cope.

William Langland

> The children were unruly and although she tried to discipline them she felt that she was at her wit's end.

COMMON IDIOM 13
The devil is in the details

What Does It Mean?

The idiom "the devil is in the details" means that if you're not careful small details can trip you up or cause you problems.

A funny illustration of the idiom "the devil is in the details"

The original phrase was "God is in the details," which meant that people should be truthful in every detail. There are different possible origins for the devil version of the idiom.

A man reading thoroughly a document

In the 1800s, the famous German philosopher Nietzsche wrote "the devil is in the details" but he wrote it in German not English.

Friedrich Nietzsche

A Sample Sentence

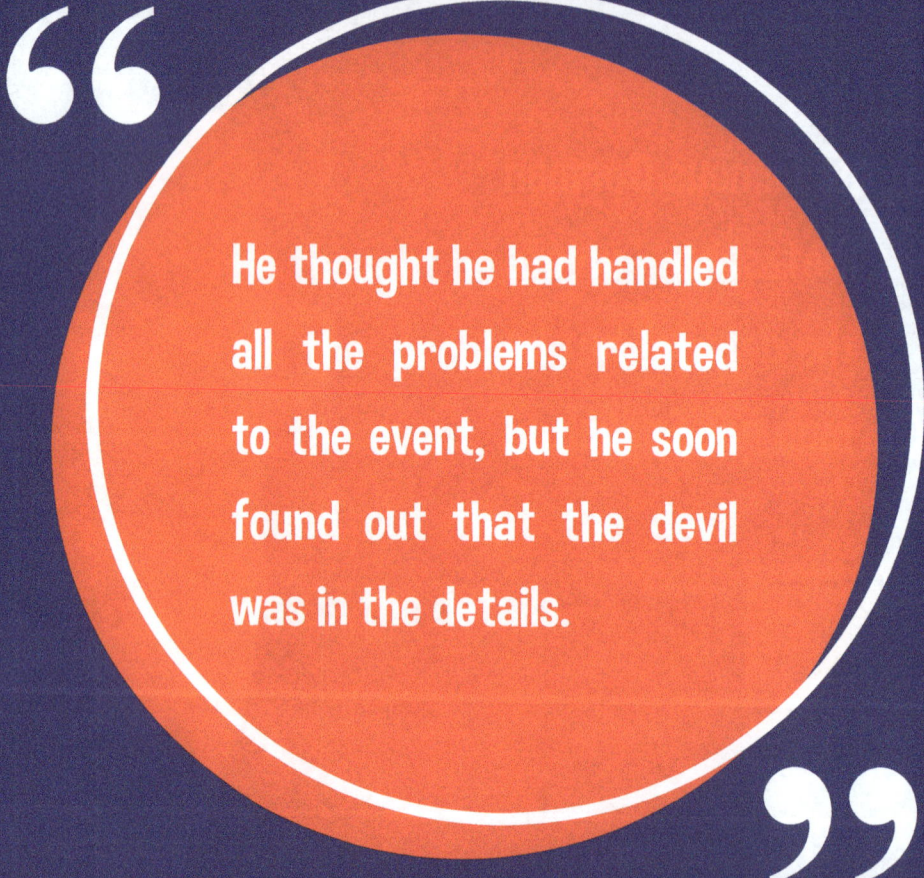

"

He thought he had handled all the problems related to the event, but he soon found out that the devil was in the details.

"

SUMMARY

An idiom is a group of words that has a different meaning than the normal definition of those same words. Every language has idioms and the English language is no exception. Many of the idioms in common use today have been in use for centuries. Some of the idioms can be traced back to historical events, but some of them have unknown beginnings or more than one path leads to their use. Just like all other aspects of language, idioms evolve and change over time and new ones get introduced to our daily language frequently.

Awesome! Now that you've learned about some common idioms, you may want to read about one of the masters of the English language in the Baby Professor book, Behind the Shadows of Romeo : A William Shakespeare Biography Book for Kids | Children's Biography Books.

Visit

BABY PROFESSOR
EDUCATION KIDS

www.BabyProfessorBooks.com
to download Free Baby Professor eBooks and view our catalog of
new and exciting Children's Books

Lightning Source UK Ltd.
Milton Keynes UK
UKHW050932110520
363081UK00002B/16